GROWING OLD IS NOT FOR THE MEEK

GROWING OLD IS NOT FOR THE MEEK

(MY AGING MEMORIES)

WALTER SAWYER

CITIOFBOOKS, INC.
3736 Eubank NE Suite A1
Albuquerque, NM 87111-3579
www.citiofbooks.com
Hotline: 1 (877) 389-2759
Fax: 1 (505) 930-7244

Ordering Information:
Quantity sales. Special discounts are available on quantity purchases by corporations, associations, and others. For details, contact the publisher at the address above.

Printed in the United States of America.

| ISBN-13: | Softcover | 978-1-963209-64-8 |
| | eBook | 978-1-963209-65-5 |

Library of Congress Control Number: 2024902791

Table of Contents

Acknowledgement ix

Introduction xi

Chapter 1: In the Beginning 1

Chapter 2: Raising Children 12

Chapter 3: Kitchen Table 17

Chapter 4: In My Father's Eyes 24

Chapter 5: Later Years 29

Chapter 6: Old Fashion Values 31

Chapter 7: Firearms Care and Caution of Using Them 36

Ten Gun Safety Rules 38

Chapter 8: What It's like to Be a Father...............................42

Chapter 9: What It's like to Be a Mother............................44

Chapter 10: Military Experience..49

To Realize..51

Tomorrow Is Not Promised to Anyone...................52

My Hopeful Future Years 53

About the Author..55

MY FUTURE YEARS

Today, Dear Lord, I am 80, and there is so much that I haven't done. I hope, Dear Lord, you'll let me live until I'm 81. But then, if I haven't finished all I want to do, Would you let me stay a while until I'm 82?

So many places I want to go, so very much to see. Do you think that you could manage to make it 83? The world is changing very fast; there is so much in store.

I'd like it very much to live until I'm 84. If by them I'm still alive, I'd like to stay till 85. More planes will be up in the air, so I'd really like to stick, And see what happens to the world when I'm 86. I know, Dear Lord, it's much to ask (it must be nice in heaven), But I would like to stay until I'm 87. I know by then I won't be fast and sometimes will be late, But it would be so pleasant to be around at 88.

I will have seen so many things and had a wonderful time. So I'm sure that I'll be willing to leave at 89, maybe.

(Thank you to the unknown person who contributed to this artcle.)

ACKNOWLEDGEMENT

Special thanks to Dolores Jewell, "my editor and proofreader." She has spent many tedious/countless hours working with me to make this book possible.

INTRODUCTION

When I look back over the years, I see what I have lost and what I have gained. I have lost many friends, many that I grew up with serving in the military: worst of all, my family members I loved for thirty-one years, my wife, and my firstborn who would have carried on the family name.

All I have are the memories we shared with each other or that our children gave me. I realize that "growing old isn't for the meek." It seems as we grow old our body changes, we fall apart and the repair shop is the hospital.

I've lived my life one day at a time. I am eighty years old; I've made many mistakes and gone out of my way to take care of others. I realize my life is given to me for a short period of time. I want to leave behind something others can remember me by. My books are 400 Years *Across the Ocean* and *The Birth of America*. I hope will be my legacy.

Definition of meek: quiet, gentle, easily imposed on, submissive, shy, peaceful, docile, mild, demure, modest, humble, lowly, unassuming.

It is no lie. "Growing old isn't for the meek."

I was told that you only write about what you know about. I can vouch for that because I am over eighty years of age, raised three children with seven grandchildren and five great-grandchildren.

I have always walked with an angel on my shoulder and a dream in my heart. Whatever I have my mind on, things do come true. Many times, I have been placed in a leadership position when I'm not even trying.

I always look forward. I once told God, "If you take care of me, I will do your biddings." Maybe the twelve thousand hours of community service is my gift to him and why things have worked out in my favor all these years. I can remember a time on the road hitching.

A stranger (maybe an angel) told me, "If you want something, repeat it every day, when you get up and before you go to bed until it comes true.(As it turned out, after taking the civil services exam, I was a police officer for six years, my dream.)

Did you ever walk down a street and talk to a total stranger? That stranger (maybe an angel) gave you an answer you want. And you never even asked him for it. Who's to say what an angel is and what package is he or she in. Under the right situation, we all could be angels at one time or another, at God's decision

I look back at the twenty-five years I spent at General Motors in Framingham, Massachusetts; my wife had hounded me to move to Florida. The northern winters are just too cold for me. The winter of 1992 reinforced me to make that decision, Florida or bust.

While living in Massachusetts, I worked with the children Olympic for three years. The task was very challenging. I loved the challenge working with the handicapped children take participate in activities, though they never thought they could do.

CHAPTER 1
IN THE BEGINNING

In the beginning, there was only me, just out of the Navy, starting a new job at Dennison MFG, living at home with my parents. Like all men, I had to find my direction and a girlfriend. I was lonely, and I needed something else in my life.

Working at Dennison, I asked a coworker if he knew of someone I could date. John G told me of his cousin 4'8, 105 pounds. It was one girl I could bring home to mother. I later found out she could not cook very well worth a damn. Time would change that. Thirty years down the road, she cooked for a nursing home for thirty patients on different diets. She cooked in a middle school cafeteria, making cookies larger than a grapefruit. The students loved them.

During the next six months, we dated, and I made several attempts to set up the wedding date. We finally eloped. My mother put a wedding reception together for us one year to the day my son was born. I wonder how many girls can say they waited to be married before having sex. The morals of today have changed so much it is a sin: when parent and schools pass out condoms or have the daughter "take the pill." "Remember, everything starts at home!"

Parents have to be understanding as children undergo different stages in their life growing up. Let's start with the husband: I found when I first got married, I had to be understanding that first night and every night thereafter. There was no *king of the mountain*, the power play between husband and wife; I had to be helpful in every way. She knew little about setting up an apartment and food to purchase. Between the two of us, life together was all new.

Just married

She would repeat, "You're never home; I sit here all day waiting for you to come home."

I said, "Go out, and get a job, and earn some money so we can find a better place to live." My reply was "as long as I put a roof over your head, clothes on your back, and food on your table." I don't see what you have to complain about. My education was the ladder I had yet to climb; I left school when I was in the tenth grade.

When she became pregnant, life changed. She cried for no reason. I could not do anything right. All I know is I had to be understanding. My stepfather and I had many talks of what was expected of me. My mom was in the shadows doing the same thing, encouraging me to be patient. They were explaining what was going on in her body, and that thought of her shape concerned her.

It took several weeks before things quieted down. The baby started kicking; her body was changing and getting bigger. The baby brought life back into our marriage. You could tell when the baby was moving. Out of nowhere, she would jump, and a surprised look was on her face and mine. Her hand would grab her stomach, and a slight noise would live up those few seconds.

Going to the delivery room, I bought a box of cigars, remembering the police officer that stopped me on the way to the hospital. I visited the Holliston police station, leaving one cigar at the main desk for that police officer, and he hadn't even given me a ticket that morning.

Sitting outside the delivery room for several hours, the nurse brought out my son who had not been cleaned up yet. I could not hold him for a dozen reasons. I was in another world; I could not wait to call the rest of the family.

My wife had babysitting jobs when she was growing up. Now she is taking care of her own baby by herself (alone most of the time) while I was at work. Occasionally, her mother or her girlfriend would come by.

During the first month, we argued unbearably as her parents had done for many years. I was ready to call it quits. One day, I just had enough. I told her to sit down, and this is the way it is going to be. No more yelling, if you have a problem, we sit down and talk about it. We don't cheat on each other. If one does, they give up everything and leave. We eventually were married thirty-one years before she died of cancer.

It's up to the parents, and it all starts when a child is born. The objective is to have them stand on their own feet and not depend on their parents when they reach adulthood.

Move to Florida Volunteer

Arriving in Florida, there was little to do, so I pick up the local newspaper to find something of interest. The Martin County American Red Cross (ARC) ran an article for help. I signed up for every course, including many state and federal FEMA courses they had in disaster area. I even went to Tampa for Hurricane Charley for several days with two other workers. When I got home, a local community refunded our expenses.

When things quieted down with American Red Cross, I was asked to help with the United Way of Martin County and the

White Dove Christmas program. My job was to set up and operate the warehouse for needy families in Martin County.

The distribution center would be working out of a closed supermarket and turning it into a warehouse for three months. My job was to oversee gathering food and toys and repairing broken bikes for children. I had about three hundred volunteers donating their time daily, from October through December twenty-three.

Working with Martin County United Way, I met someone who asked me to help out with American Association of Retired People (AARP) doing federal income tax returns. I prepared federal income taxes at no charge for members of the community till April fifteen, end of the season.

I was asked to be the district coordinator for the next ten or so years. During this period, I lost my wife to cancer, and I was on my own. We were married for thirty-one years.

I am a person who loved to help, and I was asked to join the Florida Guard Association. This gave me the opportunity to start a program serving the people in the community while helping sometimes under the police and sheriff department in these counties.

We worked with the Martin and St Lucie County Sheriff's offices at street fairs, county fairs, and two different air shows doing security and traffic control. We were also asked to do outside events with veterans and civic groups.

I know that bringing in the military, volunteer service has made all the difference in my life and has taught me right from wrong. I still make mistakes and will for the rest of my life.

Life's experiences made us into the people we are today; this will carry us to the end of the road of life. I once had a conversation with a pastor's wife and told her the same thing; boy, did she go off the deep end. She made the comment, "God made my husband into the person he is and not life experiences." When I look back, we both were correct in our own way.

Like Robert Frost once said, "When he came on two roads diverged in a wood, and I took the one less traveled by, and that had made all the difference." Raising children follows this idea. Parents take the road laid in front of them hopefully, and they do it as a team, working together.

I can remember when I was fifteen on a hand-operated 1885 fire pump on wheels. We were in a race alongside the pump when I lost foot pace. Who was it that picked me up by my pants belt, pushed me forward, and kept me from falling under the wheels? "Was it an angel?" I managed to fall into place and finish the race standing up for the fire pump hose distance race.

My parents had their own way of raising the family. My mother, if she could stay home instead of working, would; we took care of the house, family, and children. Dad was the breadwinner, and sometimes, it required more than one job for him to accomplish the task.

Two children: third

The two children waited for the new baby to come home before opening their gifts. Their mother was in the hospital having the third member of our family. I found out how much a single parent really does with two siblings, five and six years old. After her delivery, she made three more trips, back to the hospital with complications coming home for good.

Stone heads (husband and wives) get nowhere being hardheaded. It is no shame to give in. I can remember many years ago when my wife and I were arguing and she kicked off her clog across the room and into the kitchen cabinet door; what a dent she put in it or the time my wife was running off at the mouth instead of hitting her.

I put my fist into the kitchen Sheetrock wall. I put a nice dent in it; I had to repair it, and it cost me fifty dollars. Who won? Who lost?Neither of us received an award for our behavior. We

5

were young; both of us wanted to win; neither one of us did as the children walked in during our action; we had set a bad example for our children to follow.

Child visiting

What really counts are how a child turns out twenty years down the road. Case in point: my daughter visited me from Massachusetts. (My late wife had passed away many years ago. I was alone.) She stripped the bathroom wallpaper and painted it over a four-day period. She did a very professional job before returning home to teach school.

My other daughter, with her husband, came down from Tennessee and pressure-washed the house. The permanent stucco paint (the paint was mixed with the stucco in construction) needed to be washed down as well as the driveway, which also needed attention before returning home from their week's vacation.

Grandparents looking on

I love to go out and eat in restaurants, especially where young parents have their children sitting at the table without making a sound. I watch them like a hawk. I love to walk over and let parents know how pleasant it is to see children behave themselves, especially while I am eating my meal.

Parents appreciate hearing favorable comments about their children (that gives them a passing grade). I had one parent come back to tell me, "You missed our son having his feet on the table and our little girl teasing her brother." However, they did it in a quiet manner.

I have become complacent in my old age, but it is nice to visit my seven grandchildren and two of my five great-grandchildren and then return them to their parents, but it's is also sad to see them go home after a short visit.

Raising Child

The fathers' place in the family is to teach respect within themselves and take pride while growing up. Boys, more so than girls, tend to be heads of their family someday. Sons, to make the father proud, especially being able to stand on his own two feet, follow in the fathers' footsteps. Girls take the mother's role in the family with cooking, sewing, keeping an eye on her little brother from time to time as they seem to be stronger than the boys.

I can remember when my sister drove her bike and broad side of a bully, which was picking on me. He went flying and never picked on me again.

I look back to when my firstborn came into our family. It was a lot of responsibility taking care of a wife, a newborn child, never mind earning a paycheck to cover all the bills. I could not dare to fail this obligation in the eyes of my stepfather. When a wife does not work, the load of earning is placed on the breadwinner working two jobs. The wife needs to pull her weight and put the meal on the table and clean clothes on his back.

When Mike was about a year old, he loved to help Mommy with various projects like folding clothes. She also bought him a toy vacuum cleaner; he did pick up paper off the floor. As the family grew, Mike would get things for his mother. He would stay beside her while washing dishes. I am glad we had Mel-Mack unbreakable dishes as a few found a way to the kitchen floor, more often than not. We did not have a dishwasher.

Raising children

By this time, we had one boy and a girl. It was their nightly chore (it is called responsibility) every night, taking turns washing the dishes. The designated washer would clean the kitchen counter, while the other swept the floor. I often asked myself, "What is this teaching our children?"

When we got a dishwasher, we had to fight to get the table clean and put away the dishes. I even commented, "I was sorry we purchased the dishwasher. The two oldest did not get along as well." We lost ground in making them behave.

Washing dishes

My children learned responsibility to finish a project and do it properly. They learned dishes had to be clean, dried, and put away in the proper places. They learned the kitchen floor had to be swept clean after the evening meal. If the dishes were not clean, they did them over again.

You should have seen their eyes when I took a stack of dishes off the shelf and told them to do them over again. Good cleaning habits are everyone's responsibility; it saves from getting salmonella and other health problems or foodborne illnesses.

There were only four in our family; I had to remove dishes from the cabinet shelf only once. They had a time limit to complete cleaning up after finishing doing the dishes. They knew that if the dishes were not done within a certain time, the dishes would come off the shelf again.

Mike in the Navy

When my son, Mike, was in the Navy, I had the opportunity to join him aboard his ship I flew from Massachusetts to California then to Hawaii where other fathers also join in with their sons on a dependent cruise aboard the USS Tarawa, LHA 1. I had to pay $1.65 per day for my meals. After a good visit, I traveled back home with my son.

Mail call: I can remember when my son was in the Navy, and I would send him a letter. I knew what it was like to go through several mail calls and not receive any letters from home. So I started sending once a week. the paper I used as my calculators is roll paper.

About two inches wide and four feet long, I would start at one end, continue to the long end, and go back to the beginning and finish. I would then fanfold the paper to fit in size-ten envelope.

My son told me how the guys responded seeing all the paper fall out of the envelope onto the deck, never mind trying to find out where the letter started. The next time I wrote on toilet paper. It was very thin and a little more difficult and time-consuming. That's okay. I had fun, and it was for my son.

After sending several letters, my son begged me not to continue as every time he got mail, the guys would gather around him. He did say it lightened up and made his day.

I can remember the time I took a military transport from San Bernardino to Tennessee. There were two of us traveling to Massachusetts. He took a bus, and I used my thumb. Along the way, our trails crossed twice. At the Greyhound bus station, I walked by waiting for his bus to depart.

A Black couple with family stopped and picked me up. They asked if I had eaten. I replied, "No." They stopped at a restaurant but refused to go in as there was a sign "White's only," which allowed me time to eat, so they sat in the car, and they waited for me to come out. We went for another hundred miles before we departed. I got a taste of what it was like in the south.

I landed in Massachusetts ten minutes ahead of George S. I called his home, and he still hadn't arrived yet.

I came home because my sister was getting married in three days. The day I arrived, I was so tired that when I backed out of the driveway, my left car door caught on the grass banking along the driveway, forcing the door to wrap around to the left front fender; what a mess! I was on the way to pick up my father at his shop. I had to tie the door frame to the door post with my belt.

When it came time to return to California, I just walked out the front door, stuck out my thumb in Navy dress uniform, and got a ride to the Massachusetts Turnpike. There I lucked out because he was also going to Ohio.

Remember, it was December. In Massachusetts, we had no snow. I wasn't so lucky in *Ohio*, and there I stood in cold temperature and strong wind. I only had on my black Navy dress uniform and a summer spring coat. I froze my backside off. I must have stood out there for over an hour before I got a ride to Los Vegas. When I left home, I had only twenty dollars in my pocket.

By the time I got picked up in *Ohio*, the money was gone. I was lucky that the driver took pity on me and gave me one meal. I eventually arrived at the air base in California a day later. I left my car three weeks ago with the permission of the base police. I made it back the ship after my leave.

Mike

I looked back and remembered the two times that my son saved my life. I was not there to help him when he needed me. He had committed suicide. I lived in Florida, and he lived in Massachusetts.

Mike had saved my life when we were scuba diving at Race Point, Provincetown, Massachusetts. An onlooker tightened up my scuba tank straps, freezing my shoulders in a fixed position, backward. Thank the good Lord that I was on the shoreline when this happened.

I let out one yell for Mike; he pulled me back to the shoreline. Another time I was driving my Army truck, I used to haul firewood. I had blurred vision in traffic. I drank two shots of Greek liquor called ouzo. It took hold of me by surprise, and he directed me through the traffic to the side of the road.

When I look back on the day of his birth, the number of time we worked together in the woods cutting firewood and then in the Navy, I asked, "What happened to all those years?"

Sudden death

My nightmare started when my sixteen-year-old granddaughter called me and told me, "Mike is dead!" He shot himself in the chest with his gun. He would have celebrated his twenty-fifth anniversary the next month.

Maureen's death

By now, I had lost my wife due to cancer and my firstborn because of stupidity. I can still see me walking around the pantry and China closet cabinet in the center of the kitchen. Time and time again, I would look for Maureen. Never mind going from room to room, that was ours for the last twenty years.

CHAPTER 2
RAISING CHILDREN

I have been told the first six years are the children-growing years, also the years to train a child. Believe it or not, you train a child the same way you would a dog or other animals. No, I am not calling your children animals, but stop and think of what I am trying to say.

They both want attention, love, and unlike cats, for example, want to please their owners, and so do children. Once you start training, *do not stop or give in*—you may change something if you see it doesn't work, but do not stop training or caring for them.

As the family grows, the first child feels like they are the king of the roost by getting all the attention until there is a new baby coming into the family. The child may feel they are pushed away with the pressure of the new addition. Feeling the mom's stomach every now and then keeps the child interested in the new member entering the family. Jealousy is just around the corner with the new addition. A child will have a thousand questions, and Mommy should answer the best way she can.

The real training starts with the young ones. Mom has many chores to do. There are diapers to be changed, and Mom needs help. Mom is the teacher; a year down the road, it will pay off by keeping Mom from working all day and night.

Two children at home

My wife had stayed in the hospital for three days before coming home. I discovered with two children and a third coming into the family, bringing home a favorite toy for each one changes the atmosphere in the home. The way my children responded was, they looked at the baby and disappeared to the other room to play with their new toys. The new baby no longer caused them to feel left out. Now the baby is accepted into the family like it was always a member of the family.

Police job

I served as a police officer for six years. During that time, I came across two little girls who came up to me, their parents being present and extended their hands upward. I know what they wanted, so I asked the parents if it was okay to pick them up. They gave their approval, so I extended my hands and picked one of them up.

Her arms just about choked me around my neck with her hugs. It felt so good making them happy. On the other hand, why was it so important for them to get love from me and not their parents? They were missing something, the need for *love*.

I presented this situation to a physical therapist, and she said, "Some people will attract children for one reason or another. It doesn't necessarily mean they are mistreated or neglected."

As a Shriner, the saying goes: *No man can stand so tall, as to lean down to pick up a child.*

Choosing a partner:

> 1. Have a mutual understanding between each other when we had children:
>
>   A. Work together.

13

B. When one parent makes a decision, the other should agree with it.

2. Comments between parents are discussed (out of sight of the children) not in front of them.

3. Don't let children use one against the other; being bullheads will not accomplish anything.

Raising children

- Phase one: lay out the rules of life. Set boundaries. Everything begins at home!

Build child esteem. I can remember when my stepfather suggested we play checkers. He told me before I made my first move on the checkerboard, "You play to win." You have to beat me in order to win; I will not give in to let you win. When I look back on what my father told me, "life is not easy; nothing is given to you." When I did beat him, I felt good and had pride in myself.

Phase two: give children the tools to work with: it is never too early to start reading to them. Sit down with your child. Hold them in your arms while reading to them. Teach them how to read. Have them read aloud to you. Read to them at a very early stage. Believe it or not, I never learned to read well until I was in the military when I was seventeen years old.

Phase three: make them a part of the household.

At a very early age, make them responsible for cleaning their room, setting the table for supper, serving the food, clearing the table, and washing the dishes. Eventually, they will take over some of Mom's work. I discovered my children behaved better when they washed the dishes by hand rather than when they stacked the dishwasher. They behaved better, and the work was done quicker— no dishwasher for them!

Phase four: practice good health habits— washing hands, brushing teeth, combing hair, etc.

Boys are different from girls. Each has different responsibilities.

Children Relationship: First Child

Two children at home

While taking physical therapy, the therapist commented that her daughter each night says, "Good night," to the mommy's baby then to mommy. In the morning, she does the same.

Grandparent

I asked my great grandson's guardian why is he acting as a grown-up? She replied, "I talk to him as if he is an adult, no baby talk at the age of five. He is polite, respectful and does not run around like a wild one." We talked to him from day one; we make him do chores: like clean up his room, help in the house including setting the table and doing chores throughout the day.

The other day, I was walking in a grocery store and watching a mother walking in front of the child pushing the food cart. I commented, "This is mommy's little helper." My thought was, *She wants to be part of the family too.* I can remember when my sister, at the age of ten, was growing up, my mother showed her the checkbook when she was writing out checks, that is, paying the bills.

Raising children, cutting the grass

I can remember when I had my daughter cut the grass in the front yard. The results needed attention, so I showed my daughter, at twelve years old, how to cut the grass, first one way then to cross one way over the other. Don't you know that many years later, she loved to cut grass and it was done perfectly? She refuses to allow her husband to touch the mower now.

Chores

I was brought up doing the same chores with the same guidelines. It didn't hurt me, and looking back over the first ten years, it paid off rather well.

My stepfather had a hobby of raising rabbits. Don't you know that at the age of ten, I was the lucky one who helped clean the cages and under the narrow gage wire? The top had one kind of wire, and the bottom had a different one. Every other day, they had to be washed down and cleaned. I refilled the food dishes daily. The droppings also had to be removed and cleaned up; I learned to respect my stepfather's wishes. In the long run, it paid off.

The interesting part was raising rabbits and the process of new baby rabbits being born. The mother would remove the hair from her chest to make beds for the little ones. Then the process starts all over again: mommy and daddy rabbits making new ones. My father kept the mating records. We sold them at Easter time as pets and took them back when the family found it was too much work. Those were the rabbits we ate.

Raising children: driving

When it was time for my young adults to drive, I made it very clear, "If your vehicle breaks down and you need help, call me, and I get there; you better be there. If you are not, I will never come to your aid again." Through the years, that rule was followed. I never turned down my kids when they called for help.

For example, my son broke down in Providence, Rhode Island. He was twenty miles away. My son fixed the car and got it running. He refused to leave the location even when his friends encouraged him to. I showed up an hour later and then followed him home.

CHAPTER 3
KITCHEN TABLE

I can remember when my wife would make supper. We sat at the table waiting for her to join us. The rule of law was, "no one was allowed to eat one mouthful of food until she sat down, and we all ate together."

On the other hand, once she sat down, if anyone wanted something, they had to get it themselves. For example, I went to my aunt's house over the holiday. We would be finished eating, and the cook, who served the food, would be eating alone. I felt sorry for her. She did all the work, and no one waited for her.

Raising children: follow parent's habits

I did notice one thing. I had the habit of choosing one type of fork because my hand was so big. One day, I noticed my kids were looking through the drawer for their own style of fork. Kids follow their parents' actions!

Family meals are a time to talk to each other: a neutral time and to express their own feelings. I worked during nights at my job and saw very little of my kids during the week. When we were

17

together on the weekend, Saturday and Sunday were a very special time.

Story: We had two children with a third on the way. Because of a mechanical device used that brought on a miscarriage, the doctor required my wife to carry the fetus to term. My family started to pull apart; the two children's grades fell, and their conduct was also unacceptable. The school called and wanted to know what happened at home. We explained the situation.

Three months later, things started to gradually get better. We learned to put my loss in the past. The family is pulling in the same direction, that is, together and operated as it did before our loss. We named the loss Jeffery, and to this day, when we talk about our third child, he is referred to as Jeffery. It seems to lift one spirit after our loss. The school called and said, "I don't know what you're doing." Things are going better now. Keep up the good work."

Grandparents

While at Bascom Palmer Eye Clinic, we were talking to two ladies across the room. One lady made a comment about what she did to her son at the age of two or three. She had him stand in the corner with his nose against the walls.

She now regrets this action when she heard from her son what he was doing is the same but to a younger grandson. The mother tried to cover up her action with the comment, "It was only for two or three minutes." A scar is laid on the soul of her son, now onto the grandson for his lifetime.

Second wife

I find it necessary to write this story because I see the next generation being almost forced into nonexistence. Drugs are taking our children away from us and from being responsible adults tomorrow.

We just returned from vacation with my wife's granddaughter who has lost her four children indirectly because her father threw her out of the house at sixteen. She had to live on the street and became involved with drugs. Today, she is living with two types of hepatitis.

Another of my wife's' granddaughters (I first met while she was in a hospital's prison drug section) for sixty days was "drying out" from an overdose of drugs. When she checked herself in, they gave her the option to check herself out whenever she felt like it. Six months later, she was found lying on the floor for twelve hours, unconscious, and now has to depend on dialysis every three days I last heard. We sit and wonder when she is going to die.

Mistreatment of a child promotes violence in later years.

Watch for children mistreating cats and dogs.

Listen to the teacher if a negative comment is made about your child. It is not a crime to have a child in trouble. It is what you do with the information afterward!

In school, follow what I did: go to school, and listen.

Parents should evaluate what other parents say about their children.

It takes an entire community to raise one child even today!

Comment: It is too often that the way we treat our children, they may carry that practice onto the next generation (There are *no direction on how to raise a child*); we figure things out as we go along.

Manner and guidance: being a parent or a friend, you cannot be both. Remember, you are the one raising the child.

Teaching children to cook

You do not have to be a child to learn to cook. My mother taught Maureen (my future wife). She had never been allowed to be in the kitchen. Maureen raised her girls as her mother-in-law taught her to be a part of the family. At harvest time, they had fun making apple pies for the freezer. I'm still alive from my daughter's cooking. I was in the army, and everything tastes good even if it doesn't.

Be flexible: my daughter had the upper hand

Be willing to accept changes. For example, I ate a crow when my daughter proved to me there is a difference between sliding and sledding; which word was correct was my dilemma. She loved to remind me of the difference, and I had to sit there and listen to it.

Table manners

No one eats a meal unless the lady of the house or cook sits down to enjoy the same meal together.

Setting rules and boundaries

I set the rules on receiving phone calls at late hour, nine o'clock. My daughter thought this was unacceptable as her girlfriends were allowed to receive call till eleven o'clock. I just didn't want to hear the phone ring all hours of the night.

Spending time together

We made plans for camping; our children traveled from the age of one till in their late teens. We traveled from Massachusetts, to Florida, to California, and to Mount Rushmore, South Dakota. We spent time on the seashore camping and fishing with the truck camper. We also traveled from Washington, DC, the monuments and Smithsonian Museum.

Extending a helping hand

While driving from the St. Lawrence Seaway, traveling over a mountain, there was an old couple broken down along the country road. I stopped and assisted the husband with his radiator; it had sprung a leak. The nearest house was five-plus miles away. In those days, I had a heart of gold. I worked on the vehicle and helped where I could.

Leaving the area, we had a practice of counting heads; one was missing. That is when I found out Michelle got looking for her, no luck. A passerby had picked her up and called the state police. In the meantime, I went down the mountain road at a high speed to the first house I saw. I ran up to the door, sprung thru it yelling, "Where is the phone?"

I called the police, explaining to them I lost my Michelle; within ten minutes, a cruiser had already retrieved her. My daughter was in his back seat. The officer must have thought I did it on purpose. He really put me through the wringer. The same thing had happened to my sister twice, same child, while they were camping.

My daughter didn't speak to us for over a week. Today, she is a schoolteacher for over twenty-five years and very particular in her work.

In our travels

Prehistoric diggings: I love to travel the back roads of our country. If I see a sign, I make a turn. Case in point: while traveling in Nebraska, I saw a sign about a prehistoric digging. I drove a few miles into the wilderness and saw a building. I can't remember if we paid any fee or not.

Inside the building was a deep hole with sign labeling the animals, in steps, going down telling us what they were and how old they were estimated to be. Surprisingly, the animals found were camel, rhinoceros, and mammoth—elephant that now exist only in Africa and not in the United States of America.

In the local area are mounds where animals had fallen into a swamp pit. They remained there causing the pits to swell and calcifying the animal bones. They are called calcium pits. Most of the pits will never be dug because there are too many of them.

Pioneer Village: While traveling in upper-state Nebraska on route 80, I stopped at a local food store for supplies. The cashier told us of a site to see called "Pioneer Village." They had camping facilities and place of historic western communities. Walking into the museum, there were three types of structures.

One was a sod cut into blocks laid on top of each other, a pioneer one-room cabin. It had a 1212 with a white sheet hovering overhead hanging from the ceiling, making it light inside to house a family of six or more. There were two types of wood log cabin, the standard log on log with windows cut out, glass windows, and the dove-tail log cabin, similar to dove tail drawers with windows. All was collected by the owner and traveling central western states, sending valuable items home.

This vast group

We camped in the campground and followed the signs into a very long building where there are hand-pulled carts—by Moran's, Conestoga wagon, oil tanker wagon, and a variety of other types of wagons used in the old west, including Vardo, a gypsy wagon. They are very rare as the madam was cremated in them. We spent a day and a half before moving on.

The most pleasant site was *Independent Rock* where three points meet for Pioneers to leave their mark on the way to California, Mormon, and Oregon trails coming from St. Joseph, Missouri. Pioneers would leave their initials carved on the rock dating back to July 4, 1830.

Give a child a hug

If your child goes to someone else to be picked up, ask yourself, "Why? What have I done wrong?"

Story: A child is picked up and brought to a convent for children. The child tells of his mother kicking him out of the house for snoring. The whole family is behind this action, including the father. The child says, "He is woken up every hour and never gets night's sleep. The child is very heavy all the time. (I was a Department of Social Services volunteer caseworker.)

Once a child is given over to the Catholic sisters, they put him in a room of his own. The child is a new person after a few days of getting a night's sleep. The sister took the child to a doctor, and he suggested the child be put on a diet to lose some weight.

Overview: What is the real problem here? The parents allow him to eat whatever he wanted; the child who is eating potato chips, French fries, or other unhealthy foods puts himself in this current condition. The parents didn't control his diet, keep him from overeating, and see that he gets the proper exercise to stay healthy.

CHAPTER 4
IN MY FATHER'S EYES

I look back over the years. I made many decisions; I do so in my stepfather's eyes. "What would he think of me?" That goes back to Mike feeling his oats, trying to take over the house. I had to stand firm. Mike was only fourteen. I had to be a stone wall to keep him in line.

He really was never disrespectful only trying to push to see how far he could get. My wife once said, "Go ahead and strike me. I know you want to. What will your father do when he gets home?" She went ahead and pushed him. He just stood there and took her aggression, and he did nothing.

One time he asked me to borrow my new pickup truck. He wanted to help his friend move. I said, "No," because of the responsibility, damage to their furniture. When I got home, the truck was gone. I waited for him to come home. He walked in the door, I took him on hitting him in his arms; he was sixteen or seventeen at the time; he played football. I did not believe in hitting him in the face, only the arms. I later found out he had only gone to the store.

Another time when I was home recovering from a job injury, my back was out of service, and it had been laid up for two or

24

three weeks. He became stone-faced, daring me to follow up with a comment. The next thing he knew, he was on the porch floor looking up. I comment, "Now what were you saying?" I suffered for a week. I don't know who got the worse of it. I could not give him an inch. In my father's eye, I wanted him to have respect for me and his mother.

My stepfather sets the direction I would travel

My stepfather was a boxer trainer for Rocky Marciano, and his arms were bigger than most men's thighs. He did not have to yell or show any force; he just looks at me, and I would shiver in my boots. He once held me at arm's length and asked who was boss. There were no arguments.

My stepfather was a strong person; I looked up to him with the utmost respect. He never swore nor hit us kids. His mannerism was in his voice. He never hit my mother in all the years they were together. He always worked at least five days a week. I followed in his footsteps, in my work habits; I worked at least two jobs for over twenty-five years.

My stepfather took the place of my real father. He was a strong influence on me from the time he married my mother. I was six at the time. He talked to me about joining the military every time we got together over the next ten years. He encouraged me by saying, "This is your country, and you must register for the draft or join any branch of the military at the age of eighteen."

I entered the US Navy at the age of seventeen and a half on a minority cruise (term of service to be discharged at twenty-one). It was the best thing I could have done. It opened a lot of doors for me while closing my past life.

I had a hard time reading in school and remembering things. I left school at sixteen. I was politely told that I was reading well below my grade level. In those days, there were no guidance programs like there are today. I was told that I will not pass this year: "You might as well quit school and save all of us the problem of failing you."

I pulled up my own bootstraps.

When I got out of the Navy and was married, I went ahead and got my GED through one of the local high schools. I went on to attend Franklin's Community College and several other colleges to acquire fifty-eight credits.

I attended Boston University for additional employment education, forty hours, along with teaching at Indian River Community College for the Internal Revenue Service, income tax on computers, certified grant specialist, forty hours, and Otis Air Force Base, military instruction, Massachusetts.

I also served with the Massachusetts National Guard and was transferred into the US Army to serve in Saudi Arabia, Operation Desert Storm.

Parent's responsibility to protect the children

As my children were growing up, each had their own problem in school. One had an issue with her fifth-grade teacher, being too free with his hands, and she refused to return to his classroom. After I visited the principal's office and we talked with the teacher, she still would not return to the room.

She finished the school year outside the principal's office as the teacher would have to bring her assignments to her each day. Today, she has been a fifth-grade teacher for over twenty-five years and is requested by many parents for their children to be in her class.

My other daughter had a smoking problem. The vice principal would catch her smoking. She was sixteen-year-old eleventh grade student who loved to smoke during the school day. After about two weeks of visiting the principal's office, she could not be punished without me being present. On the last visit my daughter called to my attention, she had permission slips to visit the girl's room.

I asked the principal why she came into this office when she had the slip. I was ready to go to the school board about his conduct; he was the vice principal. He was speechless and consented to send her to the school for problem children. The problem was resolved, and there was no more future incident with my youngest daughter that school year.

My son told me, later in years, that I had gone to school because he gave the teacher a hard time, and I took him over my knee in front of the class and spanked him. I do not remember this incident at all. Today, I would have been in trouble if I did.

I do remember the time, at the dinner table, when my youngest daughter was out of line. I took my fist and placed it on the kitchen table top. (Remember, I never ever hit my kids.) And my daughter thought I was going to hit her; placing her hand in the line of fire, I hit her hand with mine.

The next day, she went to the school nurse and told her what I did. Great balls of fire!

The school nurse reported me to the state, and I had a social worker visit my home. We sat at the kitchen table with the deputy chief of police/deacon of the Catholic school my kids went to. Needless to say, I won my case. I won't elaborate on the comment said that day on my behalf.

I ended up as a volunteer caseworker for the State of Massachusetts, social service. The first day I walked into the office I was assigned to, sitting at the desk was the social worker who visited my home. We never said a word to each other.

Children's place in the family

I always wanted a new pickup truck. The pickup truck I had was an old Willys Jeep, and I could not do much with it. When I got my new pickup 1976 GMC three-quarter ton full-time four-wheel drive, I thought I was in heaven. I purchased a Corsair truck camper, and we would go to the sand dunes for the weekend at Provincetown, down the cape. Before we left, I would have to change my work tire—(knobby tires) to street tires, off on Friday and back on Monday.

Teaching my children to drive

Both of my kids learned how to drive when they were seven or eight years old. One time, I was putting on the camper into the bed of the truck. I started to lose it. Mike and I grabbed the camper, and I told my daughter to back the truck up while we held onto the camper. Like a champ, she put it where it belongs. It would have been a total loss if she failed, and maybe one or both of us could have gotten hurt but families who work together stay together.

I used to cut firewood, and I had three army ten-wheel tire truck to haul my firewood. Many times, I would have my two children with me; it was an automatic transmission, while we were in the woods. Driving in the woods was like a maze. It was only dirt or paths between cut tree stumps. They thought it was heaven driving the truck.

CHAPTER 5
LATER YEARS

Every time I talk with my children over the phone, at the end of the conversation, "I tell them I love them." Sometimes during my early years, I never remember my father saying or me hearing these few words to me. "I love you."

Children growing up

Parents set the guidelines when giving children the lead. Allowance (not money) is given to encourage children to help out with chores around the house, making it easier for the parents. Parents can be flexible and understanding to a point; when unnecessary and matured pressure is applied, the atmosphere can change.

The one thing parents cannot do or should not do is give in. Changes can be made down the road to correct the situation. Remember, not every decision will be the correct one; you can only do your best.

Getting along

Being married for so many years, husbands and wives run into conflict from time to time. In front of the children or in public, it is hard to say, but conflicts should be handled, on the side, alone. I have found disputing with my better half is to give in; let the air cool off. Then casually bringing up the issue at a different time gives us a chance to discuss the subject a little at a time.

CHAPTER 6
OLD FASHION VALUES

I took the following off the Internet. *Eric Kreye* covered the issue so well. I thank him for expressing himself. I could not pass up this well-versed Old Fashion Value address (Something Wrong Today by *Eric Kreye, verse* "Old Fashion Value," John August Kreye).

Whatever happened to family values—good, old-fashioned honesty, respect, purity, caring, and commitment? Today, nearly half of the families in America have been shattered by divorce; children are home alone, while parents work. Guns are readily available. Crime is commonplace. Sex outside of marriage is accepted; truth is relative, and the focus is on "what's in it for me?"

To add further confusion to our society, there are regular graphic descriptions of sex, crime, and killing on television and the printed page. A few years ago though, newscasters would have blushed to report such things. Add to this the strong popularity with our kids of video and computer games that glorify killing. Is it any wonder there is no respect for life anymore?

The restraints on sex before marriage have almost disappeared today. In an effort to control the rampant number of teenage pregnancies, many schools are offering free condoms to any teen who wants them. The result of one survey shows that parents and

31

students are more than two-to-one in favor of such distribution. According to one article, more than half of high school teens are sexually active.

In recent months and years, there have been several nationally reported shootings in high school where teens have randomly killed other teens.

What's happening? Who's to blame?

Of course, ultimately, Satan is to blame. It is his studied plan to bring everything possible to bear on the inhabitants of earth that will cause them to turn far away from God. Besides, this satanic power enjoys hurting, maiming, and killing humanity in the most degrading way, thereby bringing sorrow to the tender heart of the great God of love and compassion.

Could it be that our families themselves must share responsibility for the woeful state of our society today? Have we as fathers and mothers in our homes allowed the society around us to dictate our values and standards? Our kids are depending on us to guide them in the right direction.

It has been said that most homes are run on three shifts—father on the night shift, mother on the day shift, and the children shift for themselves!

Recently, Randy Maxwell wrote an "open letter to parents everywhere" that appeared in his local paper, in which he shared some thought-provoking comments. Here are a few excerpts:

As much as we want to blame Hollywood, the music industry, or whatever, we have to blame ourselves for allowing our culture—a culture that is drunk on violence and se—to poison our children. We must protect our own children. Nobody else is going to do it...

There's no mystery here, parents, we've systematically permitted our violence-addicted culture to program our children through the cartoons, movies, video games, and music we pay for and allow them to ingest…

We've allowed strangers into our homes—strangers who have taught our children that killing is cool, that guns are power, that death is funny and to be watched with a Coke and a bag of popcorn…

You and I are going to have to take action to protect our kids. You want to cut the violence in our culture? Stop buying it for your kids.

I'm calling on parents everywhere to go on a nationwide boycott of violent records, violent movies, violent video games, and violent cartoons. If your kids have slasher and shoot-'em-up video games get rid of them. If they have posters on their walls of rock, rap, or metal groups that glorify rape, sodomy, suicide, and drugs, take them down… Turn the channel from cartoons or programs that feature violence as something to laugh at.

And by the way, parent, that means you will need to boycott the body-blasting features yourself too. Kids won't tolerate hypocrisy. If it's bad for them, it's bad for you. If you're going to boycott some of it, boycott all of it.

This may all sound rather simplistic and naive, but listen: Filmmakers and record producers and Game Boy execs rush violent products to market for only one reason—because people buy them. People like us…

Though we can't stop people from producing garbage, we can stop our children from eating it.

And if enough children stop eating it, there won't be any whatever.

According to the December 9, 1991, issue of U.S. News and World Report:

Since the late 1970s, Americans have been gradually rediscovering the importance of family values... New polls show that this yearning for the stability of the past is at least partly driven by a growing belief among Americans that they have less control over their lives and those of their loved ones. About 8 in 10 Americans say they acquired their core values from the family, according to a new survey... But two thirds say, unhappily, that today's children are getting their values from television, movies, musicians or music videos.

This seems to confirm the old saying "garbage in, garbage out." What our minds feed on is what will influence our actions sooner or later.

What can be done to change all this? Perhaps if we each determine to make a difference in our own lives, our own homes, a positive change will come in our society, a change for the better. Some of the good, old-fashioned values of the past can be recaptured.

Here are some suggestions that will help bring about some much-needed change in our families:

Spend time together. Love and time are what a child wants most today from Mom and Dad. Even doing routine tasks together will never be forgotten such as doing dishes together, working in the garden, cutting firewood, going camping, or doing some biking. You don't have to do a lot of talking but just being together.

Set definite limits. It may mean some tough love and discipline at times. Did you know that kids dislike teachers who can't keep order? I'm sure they feel the same way about how things go in their homes.

Someone said, "Discipline is a risky form of love because the child often rejects the one administering it. However, when discipline is given fairly and in love, kids do fine." It has also been said that discipline is one of the most durable gifts we can give our children.

God spoke through the wise King Solomon. This is what he wrote:

He who spares his rod hates his son, But he who loves him disciplines him promptly. (Proverbs 13:24 KJV)

Be the right model. Live what you believe and say. Be genuine. Kids have a way of spotting hypocrisy immediately, and they don't like it. It has often been said that the best thing fathers can do for their kids is to truly love their mother—and don't be afraid to show it.

Show your kids how much you value them. Consistently, demonstrate love and respect. This involves being a good listener, speaking in respectful tones, expressing appreciation for something well-done, and showing affection (appropriate touching on a regular basis). Resist the temptation to "preach" to your kids. Think of what it takes to make you feel valued and do the same to your kids.

When appropriate, let the kids choose—but make sure they understand that each choice has consequences, good or bad. They must learn to accept responsibility for their choices. It is not always the loving thing to shield them from suffering brought on by their own choices. Often, this is the best way to learn—child or adult.

Pray! Pray! Pray!Pray for your kids and for yourself. You need God's help to make sure you do and say the right thing at the right time. And your kids need God's protection from the temptations that Satan puts in their way constantly. Someone has said that the most lasting gift we can offer our children is the gift of our prayers. It is a gift of tremendous power and will have definite eternal consequences but costs nothing but our time. May God grant that true *family values* will return to the families in our society.

Anything that effects the family should be included when talking about *family values.*

35

CHAPTER 7
FIREARMS CARE AND CAUTION OF USING THEM

I started using firearm, guns, more than fifty years ago. When I first married, within the first week of marriage, I moved into our apartment. My mother suggested I remove my play toys from her house. Maureen was very upset about me bringing home a J. C. Higgins shotgun in her house. I was heading for a brick wall as I made the comment, "Who brings in the paycheck?"

She replied, "You do." If I bring home the paycheck, whose house is it? Is it ours? I also said, "I love you very much, and I want you to stay, but the gun will stay. I hope you do too."

She replied, "You would let me leave." The issue of guns never came up over the next thirty years. (This is a true statement.)

I started teaching my son and daughter about guns when they were about five or so years old. I would take them in the basement of our home and shoot my 357 with Speers, plastic bullets. I hovered over them so it would be impossible for them to move the firearm in any direction other than the direction I wanted to shoot in.

The target was a cardboard box with a towel dropped over the front. After we shot, I would throw the towel in the rubbish barrel as it was no longer any good. They would shoot plastic bullets with a CCI Primer, large pistol; the gun would hold five shells, not six.

Teaching them firearm safety at an early age kept them from having an accident and showing their playmates. I had placed strong feeling in them not to handle my firearm at any time. At this early age, I taught the ten rules of firearm handling. They lost their interest at firearms at an early age.

I can remember when my children were ages seven or eight, saying, "Dad, let's go shooting." I stopped whatever I was doing and take them to the local sandpit for an hour or two. Whenever they were tired, they would say, "Let's go home."

Note: I don't have all the answers, so I reach out to where I can find them, the Internet. Case in point, firearms safety rule, all these rules I have worked with for years; some people explain them a little better, Russ Chastain: instructor.

Another way to say it, which Dad taught me many years ago, is, "Never point a gun at anything you're not willing to shoot."

TEN GUN SAFETY RULES

Assume that Any Gun, at Any Time, is Loaded

Guns are used safely millions upon millions of times every year, but the potential for injury and death is always there. For this reason, we need to follow basic safety rules at all times when handling firearms, including handguns like *revolvers* and *pistols*, *rifles*, shotguns, muzzleloaders, air guns.

Here are ten rules you should always follow with any firearm.

1. *Always keep your gun pointed in a safe direction.* This is the NRA's no. 1 gun safety rule and with good reason.

   The *National Shooting Sports Foundation* (NSSF) explains that you should only ever point your firearm in the direction of something you intend to shoot to avoid possible accidents.

   This rule counts for unloaded firearms as well as loaded ones, and the NSSF suggests making a habit of always knowing which direction your gun is pointing. The foundation adds, "If everyone handled a firearm so carefully that the muzzle never pointed at something they didn't intend to shoot, there would be virtually no firearms accidents."

2. *Keep your finger off the trigger until you're ready to shoot.* The NRA suggests resting your finger on the frame of your firearm, outside the trigger guard, until you are ready to shoot.

   In an article for *Guns and Ammo*, Dan Johnson points out that while this might feel unnatural, it's essential for safety.

Johnson explains that older guns, like those from the early twentieth century, had eternal hammer designs that made them safer, but bolt-action designs with hair triggers make it easier to accidentally fire your firearm. The same can be said for more modern models like glocks and Ds.

3. *Keep your gun unloaded until ready to use.* According to the NRA, if you don't know how to check if your firearm is loaded, you should probably not be using it. As with the abovementioned points, keeping your gun unloaded helps prevent accidents.

   Survivopedia takes this rule even further by suggesting that gun owners keep their firearms and ammunition separate. That way, if someone gets a hold of your firearm who shouldn't, they won't be able to do much with it.

4. *Know your target and what's behind it.* Before firing your gun, the NRA says you need to be absolutely sure that you've identified your target, but you also need to know where your ammunition will go after.

   This means you'll need to take some time to survey your environment before you fire to make sure there are no people or other unintended targets nearby.

   Hunter-ed.com adds that everything in front of you and beyond your target is your responsibility.

   The site suggests making sure you have a proper backstop for target practice and making sure you never fire at a flat, hard surface or a body of water.

5. *Know how to use your gun safely.* A firearm is a dangerous weapon and should be treated as such. Do not handle a firearm if you don't understand how it operates.

Not all firearms work the same way, and the NSSF suggests familiarizing yourself with the instruction manual before using your gun.

The NRA says you should at least know how to safely open and close the action and remove any ammunition from the gun or magazine. It's also important to remember that a mechanical safety device is never foolproof.

6. *Be sure your gun is safe to operate.* Like any other tool, your gun needs to be maintained to ensure it works optimally.

The NRA suggests taking it to a gunsmith if you have any doubts about your firearm's safety whatsoever. The same goes for guns that are old, haven't been fired in a while, or the showing visible damage or rust.

7. *Only use the correct ammunition for your gun.* All firearms are designed to work with a specific kind of ammunition. The NRA says only cartridges designed for your specific gun can be fired safely.

If you're not sure which ammunition to use, you can check your owner's manual or look for a stamp on your cartridge box.

The NRA warns that using the incorrect bullets could cause damage to your gun or even the person holding it.

8. *Wear ear and eye protection, where appropriate.* If you've ever been near a gun when it's been fired, you'll know that most firearms are loud. So loud, in fact, that the NRA says they could potentially harm your hearing.

Your best defense is a set of earplugs or muffs, but in an article for the *United States Concealed Carry Association*, Beth Alcazar writes that she prefers to use earplugs over muffs.

Alcazar suggests going for an ergonomic shape that fits your ears tightly. She says they're comfortable and inexpensive.

Similarly, firearms emit gas and debris when fired, which can damage your eyes. A pair of safety glasses that covers the sides of your eyes as well will keep them safe.

The NSSF suggests wearing eye protection while cleaning your gun too. This will guard against springs or cleaning solvents.

9. *Never shoot under the influence of alcohol, over-the-counter drugs, or prescription medication.* The NRA is very clear when it comes to anything that might impair your mental or physical capabilities: Don't mix it with firearms. The organization points out that even legal medication can have an effect, so it's best to read labels and talk to your pharmacist about possible side effects.

10. *Store guns safely.* There are dozens of ways to store your firearms, but whichever method you choose, it's imperative that no unauthorized person can access it.

This means that only you and those you trust should know where your gun is and how to access it.

Read the full article here: "10 Top Gun Safety Rules Upheld by the NRA"

Urgent: Do you approve of President Trump's job performance? Vote here now!

CHAPTER 8
WHAT IT'S LIKE TO BE A FATHER

It has been said that most homes are run on three shifts—father on the night shift, mother on the day shift, and the children shift for themselves!

When I came home from work at three o'clock in the morning, the last thing I wanted to be was woken from my sleep up at 6:00 a.m. by my children. If they woke me up, I had the two of them wash the dishes before they went to school. Even if they had a bus to catch and the time was short, they had to finish up the dishes before they left for the bus. They never woke me up again, and the house was very silent for me to sleep.

New baby

Like all new couples, just married, the first one comes anytime Mother Nature steps in. Living with the metabolic changes a woman has over the nine months is an experience in itself. A good friend of Maureen's taken me to one side and had a talk with me. It was the best thing that ever happened to me.

Morning sickness is something I had to get used to, and you'll want have to support her in every way you can. I found a way to overcome the problem; take her in your arms, two or three times a day, and tell her how much you love her. She's sensitive to her body changing, and I might not love her as much. Understanding is what she needs, and being there for her will make all the difference.

This is where you become a man. She will cry when there is no reason to cry. She will sound off for no reason, go off the deep edge for no reason. I was told to apologize for the things I didn't do right, and that had to be told to me by my father. It settled down things to a smooth atmosphere. If it wasn't for him, the first one would have been the hardest. Remember, you both are getting used to a new way of life. In all, we ended up having four.

Now she needs maternity clothes as she and the baby grow together as time goes on. In real life, she is the most beautiful creature on this earth. I love to feel the baby kicking at five months into her pregnancy as I recall.

When I brought my wife and son home from the hospital, not so much of the emptiness of the apartment changed. I was an old hand at changing diapers; my wife was green. She found out the hard way of doing Mike's gazers (he let the no. 1 fly) in her mouth or all over her while changing his diaper.

Change of pace: I would not want to be one of those men who gives up all these little pleasures without leaving a piece of me behind to carry on the family name. I'm not saying it is going to be easy.

CHAPTER 9
WHAT IT'S LIKE TO BE A MOTHER

If it was easy, there would not be any rewards for the future. Just when you think you have solved all the problems, things fall apart, and you have to start over again.

Baby joins the family: Maureen has a new friend, a friend that is her for the next six years until it leaves to start school. Maureen will care for the sibling, when it comes to changing diapers; on boys is an experience for Maureen. Little boys' have gazers when she least expect it. He shoots into the air as she changes his diaper, hitting anything in the way.

A smart mom will start training her child as soon as it can walk. Mom's little helper is her right hand in any way she can use him. Saying no is the hardest word any mom can say, followed up with enforcing it. I found a phrase: "Let's do it together"; here is a new way. Patience only comes when Mom can stay home and does not have to work.

I can remember those first six years can make all the difference on how the child will turn out ten years down the road. I started to

44

get familiar in the kitchen by helping my grandmother stir cookie dough.

Maureen (my late wife) just had her nose surgically repaired for a deviated septum when she was kicked by Mike, breaking it again. Mike was exercising his legs, kicking them in the air, as babies do. Mommy just walks around with a white plaster cast, on the nose, for the third time.

Putting Mike to bed and not keeping a very close eye on him, he enjoyed playing the part of an artist with his number two on the wall next to his bed. We had a mess to clean up, never mind the crib he was playing in.

Importance of family

I have found that when the children grow up and leave home, the world never sounded so empty. The pictures on the walls or in albums are all we have especially when you are the only one left. My life is so very empty. I started alone sixty years ago. My living children are scattered in two states several days apart. Some of us just sit in wheelchairs melting away.

Explain my early family life: I found the love and understanding, overlook the hurdles that come with raising children. The mother is the protector, and the father is the breadwinner and paid the bills.

I try to listen to my son when he puts earphones onto his radio—loud noise, scolding my son for playing his earphones loud. My son gave the phones for me to listen to; the phones were quieter than a church mouse but loud when I walked by. It drove me crazy to hear the loud noise; what else could I do?

Parents are willing to forgive their siblings just by overlooking it, positive thinking.

Parents have to be understanding as children undergo different stages and have everlasting patience. Children mimic their parent's actions. For example, look how their father dresses when he brings in visiting playmates.

Lots of family weight lie with the father; in many cases, it sets the direction the family will go. I can remember my father setting the pace for his vacation. With my family, I led the way for vacation doing over the house, putting in bay windows in the pallor and two sky lights in the kitchen for more light to come in.

The father caters to children; a father has two positions: be a friend or be responsible for what happens to the wife or children. For example, go play ball or be the umpire to oversee the others who play ball.

Love and friendship from the eyes of being a mother: the real stories

No child wants another parent if parents act like children and end up getting a divorce; the first statement children make is, what did I do to make them split up? All I know is being from a broken home, their world is shattered for the rest of their lives. Yes, they learn to live with the situation, but moving on is not easy. The scar is hidden within them forever.

Who puts laughter on a child's face? Mom and Dad who cares when they have a child.

What is motherhood? "Individual opinion."

What does it mean to be a mother? These questions are as challenging to answer as they are simple. Yes, to give birth, to adopt children, and to have a family, but being a mother is also about much more than that, isn't it?

There's some large, overwhelming, and beautiful peace at the center of motherhood that is so hard to put into words. It's a feeling, a joyful experience. Maybe that peace is best called *love*. If so, it is truly a unique love reserved for the mother/child relationship. And when you've felt it, you know it!

To me, being a mother means to see all the possibilities in the world through your children's eyes. Mothers want to be the kindest and most generous image of yourself so that your children can look up to you. On a day-to-day level, being a mother means being tired, sometimes grumpy and never left alone.

For me, motherhood is seeing the profound value in learning about who your children are, and then encouraging and teaching them to be the best versions of themselves. It is my greatest hope that this acceptance and unconditional love will empower and strengthen my children as well as foster self-confidence and kindness!(Courtney Westlake, blogger, Blessed By Brenna)

Motherhood is truly a remarkable gift and a privilege that I hold very close to my heart. To me, being a mother means to be fearless, to be a positive role model, to be a continuous cheerleader for every milestone my children will experience, to demonstrate the abundance of unconditional love that has no end and to cherish the countless memories that is truly priceless. (Eluka Moore, cofounder and author, *Kitchen Club Kids*)

To me, being a mother is the greatest job in the world. Helping my girls through all the things life throws them, while also lifting them up so they can reach for the stars and grab one! That's what being a mom is all about—always being there—the shoulder to cry on, the cheerleader to never give up, the one that gives the standing ovation, the familiar hand to hold. (Bobbie Rhoads, founder and president, FunBites LLC)

Being a mother means being completely and totally overwhelmed (in the best possible way) by love, joy, responsibility, and selflessness. Motherhood means sleepless nights, big belly laughs, and caterpillars on the coffee table, finger-painting in the kitchen, stubbed toes, and toothless grins. Motherhood has made life more colorful than I ever knew it could be. Being a mom means I have two little people who walk around with my heart and soul in the palms of their sweet, smudgy hands. (Lauren Casper, blogger) To me, being a mother means getting to see all the possibilities in the world through your children's eyes, and also wanting to be the kindest and most generous version of yourself, so that your children can look up to you. On a day to day level, being a mother means being tired, sometimes grumpy and never left alone, and then, in one funny, loving or meaningful moment with your kids, realizing that it's all completely worth it. Times one million. (Cara McDonough, blogger (father felt the same way)) Being a mother means being an emotional blankie for your children. They snuggle with you at night, run to you when they're hurt, and stand behind you in scary situations. There's nothing more warm and fuzzy. (Maia Haag, cofounder and president, I See Me!LLC (this father took care of the children and school problems))

For me, being a mother means it is MY responsibility to give my children the tools they need to live a happy and meaningful life. In the case of my daughters, Lily and Melanie, I wanted to empower them with a skill set that would allow them to create independent careers and avoid the glass ceiling…they are on their way with confidence and the sky is the limit.(Renee Sandler, founder and CEO, BLAMtastic®)

CHAPTER 10
MILITARY EXPERIENCE

I remember the time I went to boot camp at Great Lake, Illinois. I never was away from home before. I had to conform to a new way of life. I was given clothes just like the guy ahead of me and the guy behind me. I was told what to do and what to think. There were sailors from all parts of the East Coast. I had a hard time reading and remember things. I left school at sixteen.

I can remember the tents of Saudi Arabia at 128 degrees inside and the hot sands of the desert. We sleep two hours a day, every day when we first arrived in the country.

I remember when I was coming home on an MAC Flight, and we were about to land when I thought the soldier next to me dropped dead. The flight nurse, who was on the plane, told me to move, and she started CPR on the victim. The C41 wheels were touching down, and the nurse got help in resuscitating the soldier. He was rushed off the plane before any of us departed.

Every time I talk about the experience, I choke up and cannot speak clearly, flashback.

Nightmares: I remember the two planes that collided in the air, and I just stood there hopeless, watching one pilot fall about

49

one thousand feet. When my ship got to the crash site, the water was still turning over with different color water and bubbles. Flashback experience: I can remember the gooney birds landing, tumbling head over heels. It sounds like seniors bouncing around.

I can remember all the dancing at the YMCA on Friday and Saturday nights. After my wife's demise, I had something to fall back on to bring life in me. While dancing on the dance floor, I started to cry; my partner asks what is wrong. "My wife just died two weeks ago."

She said, "Cry all you want; I lost my husband a month ago."

It's no lie. Growing old isn't for the meek!

I have been taking physical therapy for over two years, two to three days a week. I notice the number of patients in the facility; two thirds are seniors over sixty. I keep coming for a different reason; I do need certain body parts repaired.

TO REALIZE

(Author Unknown)

To realize the value of a sister, ask someone who doesn't have one.

To realize the value of ten years, ask a doctor who has just received his degree. To realize the value of four years, ask a graduate.

To realize the value of one year, ask a student who failed his final exam.

To realize the value of nine months, ask a mother who gave birth to stillborn.

To realize the value of one month, ask a mother who gave birth to a premature baby.

To realize the value of one week, ask the editor of a weekly newspaper.

To realize the value of one hour, ask a couple who waiting to be reunited.

To realize the value of one minute, ask a person who has missed the train, bus, or plane.

To realize the value of one second, ask a person who has survived an accident.

To realize the value of one millisecond, ask a person who has won a silver medal in the Olympics.

To realize the value of a friend or loved one, lose one.

Time waits for no one.

Treasure every moment you have. (I thank the Fishwrapper of Lancaster County/East, Pennsylvania, edition: April 21, 2011)

TOMORROW IS NOT PROMISED TO ANYONE

(Author Unknown)

Tomorrow is not promised to anyone, Young or old alike, And today may be the last chance, you get to hold your loved one tight.

So if you're waiting for tomorrow, Why not for today?For if tomorrow never comes, You'll surely regret the day.

That you didn't take that extra time, for a smile, a hug, or a kiss, and you were too busy to grant someone, what turned out to be their one last wish.

So hold your loved ones close today, and whisper in their ear, Tell them how much you love them, and that you'll always hold them dear.

Take time to say, "I'm sorry," "Please forgive me," "thank you," or It's okay." And if tomorrow never comes, You'll have no regrets about today.

MY HOPEFUL FUTURE YEARS

Looking to be nasty at 90 I'm 91 looking for what tomorrow may bring I'm tired of being blue at 92 I want to live as long as I can and feel free at 93 I have many memories; that's what's keeping an open door for 94.

It's great to be alive at 95 and alive I'm tired of being sick at 96 I'm glad to be alive and not in heaven at 97 I'm lucky to be able to have a date at 98.

I live on my memories, all of them at 99 And now no anxieties or dread; wow, I may even make it to One H-U-N-D-R-E-D! One Hun-dread! 100!I hope it isn't The end.

What is life? Life is to climb up hill, balance till you retire, and glide to end I.e., pay off your bills before you retire!

ABOUT THE AUTHOR

The author quits high school at the age of sixteen and went to work with the advice of his stepfather. He either work or go on the street. He found a job at a local Hat Company, which lasted only a few days when the Pope said, "Women do not have to wear hats to church."

He entered the US Navy at the age of seventeen. He went to Great Lake, Illinois, before traveling to the Panama Canal and eventually the West Coast to California.

After leaving the Navy with an honorable discharge, he got married and raised three children. Twenty years later, he entered the Massachusetts National Guard and was drafted into the US Army for Saudi Arabia.

While serving in Germany, three years earlier, he got hurt; the injuries recurred while on active duty in Saudi Arabia. He was honorably discharged. He was sent home on a MAC Flight to the states. He continued to help for the next year with AmeriCorps, working for a disaster program in seven Mobile Park Communities, totaling 12,000 hours of community service.

He now enjoys the senior way of life with his seven grandchildren and five great-grandchildren.